PUBLIC ABSTRACT

Public Abstract
poems

Jane Huffman

The American Poetry Review
Philadelphia

Book design and composition: Gopa & Ted2, Inc.
Distribution by Copper Canyon Press/Consortium

Library of Congress Control Number: 2023931090

ISBN 979-8-9875852-0-7 hardcover
ISBN 979-8-9875852-1-4 paperback

9 8 7 6 5 4 3 2 FIRST EDITION

The American Poetry Review
1906 Rittenhouse Square
Philadelphia, PA 19103

www.aprweb.org

For Di

"But to say, I *know* — is there any touch in it?"
— Jean Valentine

"Pain is the ransom of formalism."
— Louise Bourgeois

Table of Contents

Foreword

I N *Public Abstract*, Jane Huffman demonstrates a steely commitment to an aesthetic vision. For Huffman, form—inventing it, bending it, subverting it, putting it to novel use, especially if working with forms passed down through time—*becomes* content: not merely expressive vehicle, but heraldry loaded with meaning.

Form in this book is also feeling: tonally cool, the repetitions and hard turns at work in these poems express with passion. They can signal uncertainty, anxiety, skepticism, inquiry, and a wish for revelatory knowing. Huffman accentuates lyric poetry's elemental qualities, where feeling is primary and the events and situations that incite feelings secondary. This, coupled with their inescapable focus on form, makes the poems in *Public Abstract* resistant to the question, "What's this poem about?"—a question that prefers explanation to experience, and one that often seeks an origin story. Huffman is more interested in the question of how experience finds style: "the 'to' escaped the darkness of the 'from'" ("Six Revisions").

Yet *Public Abstract*'s bouts with the about yield two of the book's central poems, "Three Odes" and "On Invention." Here, the poet's lived experience—with an addict brother, her sick body, the disturbances of psyche and society—come to the fore. These poems change the way I read the more form-first poems, deepening my sense of the life forces pressing the latter into play. And suddenly I feel that the stakes are high for this collection: the poems in *Public Abstract* deeply resist the autobiographical Confessional mode surging still through much contemporary poetry, but they also feel compelled by the deep psychic disturbances that characterize such writing. In "On poetry," from a clutch of haibun that close the book, Huffman writes:

> I know a little poetry. I've broken down. I've wept into the zenith of a rose. "Each tear [. . .] A globe." The way John Donne rhymes "wind" and "find" in the final stanza of OF WEEPING. I've come that close.

Close—but she always verses back from the weeping brink, keeping her wits with intellect and humor. Huffman has a wry and knowing sense of self and the art she plies; her poems can veer into unexpected, tension-breaking puns and literary jokes. After telling us she's "come that close," she ends "On poetry" on a note that never fails to crack me up:

> Ars poetica: / Yelling "representative" / into a dead line.

Wit and music are two primary pleasures of *Public Abstract*. The poems' insistence on foregrounding rhyme and refrain (exact and slant) calls to mind the phase music of Steve Reich and Philip Glass; it also calls to mind nonsense and nursery rhyme. In the most interesting ways, I sometimes cannot tell if a poem's "plot" is being driven by sense or sound, fact or sonic fabulation:

> [I reached an arm]

> I reached an arm
> Across Louise
> And doing so I made

A shape it gave
Me pause a wending
Shape an absent

Mind she said
Goes limb to limb
With the sublime

It seems that, for Huffman, revelation often comes by ear—singing reveals knowing, rather than knowing sparking song.

Huffman's devotion to repetition comes with reward and risk: in the first case, she refreshes the operations of sonnet and sestina, and transforms revision into a genre in its own right; in the second, the poems can teeter on the verge of mannerist madness. I for one wouldn't have it any other way. What bravery to write them! Completely thrilling to read them.

You can see this reward and risk at play in "Failed Sestina," a tour de force of obsessive thinking. Obsession is an experience for which the sestina, with its focus on six repeating words through six stanzas, seems primed. Huffman exaggerates the repetitions that distinguish sestina and strips the form to its core psychic potential:

When I curl up on the floor
of the cell of my want.
I bear my fear in my cells

like I'm bearing a ring.
Like I'm curled up inside
of the ring in my ear.

I rap at my want for a door
where there is no door.
A will where there is no will.

At my want for unveiling.
My will to unveil it. The curve
of my will and my ear

to the door. With the curl
of my ear to the door.

By the end of this poem I feel a tinge of dread; the last image
vibrates with suspense. Suddenly I see Huffman's kinship with
Poe—a poet who also pushed repetition and rhyme to its lim-
its (Huffman's excesses, to me, are more successful). And like
Poe's works, this poem, and many others in *Public Abstract*, feels
informed by the American Gothic tradition, which is fascinated
by disturbances of mind, by paranoia, anxiety, hallucination,
dream. In Dickinson this is never more apparent than in poem
340, "I Felt a Funeral, in My Brain,":

> I felt a Funeral, in my Brain,
> And Mourners to and fro
> Kept treading - treading - till it seemed
> That Sense was breaking through -
>
> And when they all were seated,
> A Service, like a Drum -
> Kept beating - beating - till I thought
> My mind was going numb -

I hear a ghost of these cadences—and the drama of an interior
assailed—in Huffman's "[I had a bout]:"

> I had a bout
> Of vertigo
> Inside my chest
>
> A clocking
> From within

Was bested
By the worst
Of me again

As if my body
Shook off
All its walls

And doors
And reeled
The outside in

Dickinson—her impassioned psychic venturing—is major marrow in Huffman's stylistic bones; so too Kay Ryan, and the spirit of Jean Valentine. Huffman sends shoutouts to all three at various points in *Public Abstract*. Very present for me too is another steely stylist: Gertrude Stein, whom Huffman matches in playfulness and bravado.

Huffman's feminism is a firm presence in this book: in stylistic allusions, in her musings (see "On beauty"), and as a response to both personal and national experience. In "On Invention" she confronts directly the suffering that can attend motherhood, from her own uterus to what women in her family have endured contending with "addict sons." In a book dedicated to slant engagements with subject matter, what prods this unusually explicit poem? An accident of Googling (how very Huffman!) Hearing an NPR journalist mention "deinvention," Huffman looks up the word and is led to Cicero's *De Inventione*, which sparks a meditation on making and unmaking, the learned helplessness of the medical establishment in treating "women's troubles," the facts and fables that characterize family history, and the forces leading to her decision to remain childless:

. . . Before me, three generations have parented addict
sons—Mildred, Ann, and Lynn each spending their

lives with their horns locked to their sons' horns, in
love and in agony . . . Early memories shadowed by
later ones. In the fable of my family, addiction is passed
from hand to hand like a hot coal. My brother holds it,
palm open.

Huffman's history with her brother also informs one of the
most moving poems in the book, "Three Odes," where she writes:

> I've mourned my living
> brother many years.
> This is the heavy
> table of my work. I lug
> the heavy table
> of my work around
> all day so I am never rid
> of it. I am never rid
> of it—the work
> that carries me like I'm
> a tired child sleeping
> in its arms. I sleep in
> my brother's arms.
> It takes all his strength
> to carry me.

Huffman's variation on the duplex, a form invented by poet
Jericho Brown, comprises the second section of this poem and
ends, "My brother's / death is long, and heavy / as a year. I've
mourned / my living brother all my life." Such declarations of
naked feeling are rare in this collection; when they appear, they
break the heart, and one can feel a why and wage in Huffman's
obsessive focus on form: it (s)mothers pain, the source from
which the book's formal feelings come.

With her ear to the door, what is Huffman ultimately listen-
ing for in these poems? I'd argue the calm that comes with what

she calls "surety." But she also knows that such calm in sureness is fleeting, perhaps even delusional, in a precarious era in an always precarious world, where precarity feels like the only sure thing. With intense resolve, *Public Abstract* pledges allegiance to "the mist / that follows certainty" ("Surety") even while it cannot refrain from "scratch(ing) / the itch of certainty" ("The Mosquito"). Perhaps, at the core, that's what sets in motion the rhyming, revisioning, and repeating gears of Huffman's striking debut: the drive to find something to count on.

—Dana Levin
January, 2023

Public Abstract

I swept
and am sweeping,
have slept
and am sleeping.

I heaved the head
of the mop
to the hod,
and I'm heaving.

I'm sweating,
I'm wetting
the corn
of my broom.

I'm washing
the floor
in the room
where I waited
for reason.

I reasoned,
I teased
at the edges
of reason.

1. A BOUT

The Rest

Still, I keep myself, I take
to bed. One lung is red. Cut red
flowers hung in pink water.

My other lung is out of line.
From one lung, I tell the truth.
From the other lung, I lie.
Cut pink flowers hung in red water.

Like a pain, the truth is mine.
The lie is that today I want to die.
Cut red water hung in pink flowers.

The rest of it is stillness, rest.
A soft cough into a hard pan.
A hard cough into a soft plane.
Cut pink water hung in red flowers.

[I was reticent in childhood]

I was reticent in childhood
Prepared for nothing
Testing fragrant waters
At the toilet water counter
Diagramming

Sentences
I ran the empty aisles
Of Mercy's auditorium
Annexed out of my own
Little annex made

A little art of panicking

[I thought that I could love]

I thought
That I could love
My fear could

Build with it
A desk and chest
Of drawers

Like fear was
Made of pine
And nails

And glue could
Sew myself
Into a dress

With it or
Matching set
In shocking blue

Could plait
My hair with it
Could paint

With it could
Thin my paint
With it

Could spread
It like a sheet
Onto my bed

Could slice a loaf
Of bread on fear's
Serrated edge

[I've failed already]

I've failed already
Unbegun

/

The sun already
Going down

Above
My house

And I have
Nothing done

/

I've come
Unsorted

Mortified to move
My body through

The world

In the way
That it demands

/

Demanding
As the world does

A pin
Into my hand

/

My body through
The world

Like a particle
Of sand

That moves
Forever toward

The sphere
Where it began

/

I've come
Unmanned

Inhabited

A host

/

Been coaxed
Out of my house

By fear

Idea after idea

/

As if my thinking

Flipped
And fled

My body

Out
My naked ear

/

I'm haunted
As a ghost

I've come undone

I needled
At my needfulness

Until it stung

/

I swept
As if my sweeping

Was a form
Of reading

/

Held the broom
Of sleep

Between
My teeth

Until I slept

/

And as I slept
I knew

That I was
Sleeping

[I couldn't drive]

I couldn't drive
And so I got a ticket
Tried to make
The trip alone
By train
Accompanied
By salience
And pain
The platitude
Of being moved
Through space
And time
But when I made
A go of it
And we arrived
I felt a falter
In my salience
A swaying
In my pride
And like a child
Picked it up
And carried the idea
Away and so
Instead today
In stocking feet
I tarried to my bed
And tried to stay

[There was a clearance]

There was a clearance
In my health a sudden
Voice the long arm
Of the mind
Reached toward me
With a choice she said
I made arrangements
Get up from your bed
She held a washcloth
To the swollen belly
Of my head
Whether she was life
Or death I couldn't tell
My health a dispossession
Like a sale I wasn't ill
In indecision
But I wasn't well

[I had a bout]

I had a bout
Of something
Undefined

Another rattle
In the lung
As if I stood

Under the ladder
Of my childhood
For years

Before I climbed
A single rung

/

I had a bout
Of vertigo
Inside my chest

A clocking
From within

Was bested
By the worst
Of me again

As if my body
Shook off
All its walls

And doors
And reeled
The outside in

/

I had a bout
Of something
Like a flame

A burning
In the core
Like shame

An ache the size
And color
Of a thought

Aboutness
Like a cough
I cannot shake

Three Odes

1.

I asked my brother death
About his journey
To the center of the world
Where he lost his life

In winter but bought it back
In spring with money
That he siphoned from our
Mother's wedding ring

He said my sister death
Is not as cunning as you think
He brought to me his little
Well of ink whenever I asked

And let me drink a little
From his flask of life and pleaded
With me when I left
He begged me not to leave

And so I sat with death
Beneath our mother's dogwood
Tree my brother and his
Death on either side of me

2.

I've mourned my living
brother many years.
This is the heavy
table of my work. I lug
the heavy table
of my work around
all day so I am never rid
of it. I am never rid
of it — the work
that carries me like I'm
a tired child sleeping
in its arms. I sleep in
my brother's arms.
It takes all his strength
to carry me.
With all my strength,
I lug my brother up
the hill where we,
as children, buried pill
bugs in finger holes.
My brother buried pill
bugs in the ground.
I dug them up. I dig
my brother's body
from the ground,
from beneath the heavy
table of the Earth.

He lugs around the heavy
table of the Earth,
the maple tree that grows
out of his head. The maple
tree that grows out
of his head is heavy
with the longing
of the dead. My brother's
death is long, and heavy
as a year. I've mourned
my living brother all my life.

3.

I don't know
my brother as a man.
A force of nature,
rather, like the wind
that brushes up
against the house
because it must.
He makes demands.
He carries with him
fallen leaves
and mites and owl
pellets ridden
with the shattered
bones of mice
because he must.

I didn't know
my brother as a boy.
Burgeoning, we parted
into different woods.
He, to using
his own shadow
like a mattress
on the floor
where he could pull
his body from his mind
like pulling cornsilk
off the husk. And I
to using sadness
like a broom to sweep
my shadow up.

[My head and its ache]

My head
And its ache
Close as two
Sisters

In Nicolae
Tonitza's
Painting

Two girls
With gusty
Eyes

Leaning
On elbows
Over
An open
Book

They look
Forward

Like fasciated
Heads
Of the same
Weed

They don't
Read
They are tired
Of reading

Coda

Form implies the opposite of form:
a globule, a formlessness, a letting go.
(Like fear implies the opposite of fear:
relief, approximation of the human
form built in packing snow.)

And yet, the opposite of form (relief
from form) implies the opposite relief:
from formlessness. Packing snow
made globular when thrown is blown
back to the ether of the whole: like grief.

2. REVISIONS

The Mosquito

1.

The mosquito
rejects her prime,
the summertime.
Rejects her onus
to be born in
inch-deep water.
She rejects it
like rejecting sleep.
Like sleep without
integrity. Rejects
the raft, her peers,
the itch. The inch-deep
mere. The water
deep as mirror glass.

2.

The mosquito
rejects me. Her sense,
her millisecond.
In her wake, a welt.
All summer long,
I fan myself. Gape
at the size of certain
sunflowers. Rattle
at the bolted door
between her death
and me. When she
dies, she conquers
me. I scratch
the itch of certainty.

Revision

1.

Like a crowd, a body moves without a mind. Moves without an ambit. Tilts without an axis. Pulls without a magnet. A school of fish could tell you that: the wind is more a rudder than a mast.

2.

[The] body, like the mind, moves in crowds. [A worm, or wave, or kiln] could tell you that. [The worm, a solitary iteration of the] fish. [The wave, a solitary iteration of] the wind. [The kiln is thinking itself warm.]

3.

The body moves with [crowded lines]. A worm or wave could tell you that. The worm [with the mind of a] fish. [The fish with the mind of a] wave. [The wave with the mind of a] kiln, thinking itself warm.

Six Revisions

The doctor holds my chest against the discus, listens like the fish below the ice listens to the fisherman. "Medicine," he says, "is not an exact science."

He listens like the ice fisherman listens to the fish. I breathe into a nebulizer and think about translation — inexact art. A fine, particulate mist.

Snow has fallen on
still-green grass.
daubed with yellow leaves.

―――

Three takes on a line from St. Augustine's *Confessions*. An acquaintance posted one online to the delight of followers, of *us*, and in delight, I went to the source, the lexicon: three alike, online translators, some fishy, copied, pasted, fished out of the public sphere. And each rings like a different key.

Snow has fallen
on [yellow] grass, daubed with
[still-green] leaves.

——

Poor old pear-thief Augustine, half-biographer:

1. "Where should my heart flee to in escaping from my heart?"
2. "Where could my heart flee to in escaping from my heart." [sic]
3. "For where could my heart flee from my heart?"

[Grass] has fallen
on [still-white snow] daubed
with [yellow] leaves.

————

In the first translation is a hammering. "Should" — a moral judg-
ment. An oiled object laid bare on a linen bed. "Shouldn't" tied
around the "should" with butcher's string.

In the second, a yip, a certainty, desperate in its forwardness.
"Where could?" as if the possible eluded him. To boot, denied
its final mark. The thought falling from "Where could?" like rain
from a cloud, a vanishing source.

Grass has fallen
on [yellow] snow daubed
with [snow-white] leaves.

———

"This will cut the cough off from the brain," the doctor says,
offers me a tiny cup of codeine-orange syrup. The ache escapes
like orange silk out of my orange lung. I slide into a mirror of my
feelings, my face enlarged, expanding like a sponge. I grab at it.

The doctor says, "I lost it in the war." He is talking about his
thumb.

[Yellow leaves have] fallen
on [white] snow daubed
with [still-green grass].

––––

In the third Augustine translation is a thrum: "For / where / could / my / heart / flee / from / my / heart?" The thrum escaped the darkness of the drum. No "to" this time. The "to" escaped the darkness of the "from."

Yellow leaves have fallen
on [green grass] daubed
with still-[white snow].

Failed Sestina

With my ear to the door
of my cell. And my want
like a comb in my hair.

Like a veil where there is no
veil. With a ring in my ear.
A ring in the hole in my ear.

I rap at the door of my will
and the door of my want
as to will them away. My

want like a veil on the floor.
I appear at the door of my
will with a veil in my hand

and a comb in my hair.
My want like a hole that
I bore in the floor.

Where my will is more
feeling than veil, and my veil
is more want for a veil

than a veil. I wear the comb
of my fear in my hair.
My veil is as thin as my want,

and my want is as thin
as a hair. When I curl up my
want in the curl of my hair.

When I curl up on the floor
of the cell of my want.
I bear my fear in my cells

like I'm bearing a ring.
Like I'm curled up inside
of the ring in my ear.

I rap at my want for a door
where there is no door.
A will where there is no will.

At my want for unveiling.
My will to unveil it. The curve
of my will and my ear

to the door. With the curl
of my ear to the door.

Revisions

I dressed myself
like Princess Margaret
on a grouse hunt

and took my dog
into the pouring rain.

―――

Like Yeats, "I made
my song a coat [. . .]
From heel to throat"

and walked my dog
into the pouring rain.

―――

We walked through
other people's plots
and rooms until my coat

was soaked completely
through with rain.

―――

My dog was happy
to be wet, a shadow
in the pouring rain.

―――

The neighborhood
was verdant green

and empty. Stairs
and gales and porches
streaming

in the pouring rain.
—————

We passed a single

woman and her dog,
who looked like mine.
Dressed, like me,

for walking
in the pouring rain.
—————

Yeats wrote, "let them
take it," which I take
to mean his pain —

his resolute disguise —

"there's [. . .] enterprise"
he wrote, "In walking

naked" in the pouring rain.

Ode

Andrea taught me to ride sidesaddle. I rode
in small and dizzying circles around her.
I rode around her in small and dizzying
circles. Past the mirror and past the mirror
where, one summer, she was reared off
by a stallion attacking his own flaring
reflection. One summer, she was reared
off, or almost. I rode into the acres
of our sunflowers. In the acres, the fields,
I overindulged in beauty. In the fields,
I rode. Andrea leaned on a rail, her body
a rail. Andrea leaned on the shadow
of a rail. My shadow rode around her,
the small bells of my intuition. She rang
the small bells of the saddle. I was
small and dizzying. I was dizzy. I rode
in small and dizzying circles. Andrea
taught me to ride, no stirrups. Nothing
suspending my body but intuition, the small
and dizzying circles of my body.
My intuition rode around me in small
and dizzying circles, her shadow riding
circles around me. I called her Andrea.

Sestina with Six Titles

I tried

to set my longing down, I tried.
Behind the white chalk circles
my longing drew. Neatly, I backed away
from longing, drew all of my swords
at once, my hands on the back of the head
of all my new longing.

I met

my longing
in the heat. Tired and hot, I tried
to shelter my longing's head,
draw hasty circles
in the sand with my swords
as if to signal stay away.

I traveled

with my longing, far away,
folded and packed my longing
alongside my shirts and swords,
and as we walked, I tried
recalling all my longing's circles
from the circles inside my head.

I rode

my longing like a horse, my sword
like a lasso stirring above my head.
I lassoed my longing, tried
to break my longing away
from its wildness, but longing
ran the fence, circle after circle.

I lost

myself inside my longing's circles,
fell into my longing like a sword
into the sea. My longing
lost itself inside my head,
and so I tried to find a way
to set it down, I tried.

I sought

to steal my longing's head,
steal language of longing away,
watch the bloodied circles
seep from the neck of my longing.
Many times, my longing tried
to kill me with my own sword.

dune after dune, the blousy heads
of onions wishing my longing away;
the horse tried; the mirage of the horse tried.

Revision: Sonnet

1.

I found a sequence in my way idea
where there was no idea before
and plucked it up as if it was already

mine an interruption like a sequin
that fell off my sleeve in childhood
and through the sieve of time

2.

I found [a pattern] in my [path ideal]
where there was no [ideal] before
and [tucked my arm into the crook

of hers] as if [she] was already mine
a [stipulation like a fracture in the spine
a rupture in the sleeve of] time

3.

A [frequency was] in my way [I heard]
a line I didn't [hear] before and [took it
down] as if it was already mine

[a modulation blatant as a rhyme as if
a bead] fell off my sleeve in childhood
[and landed in my mind]

Surety

I'm sure as wetness
follows steam.
I'm sure as cold
that follows
wetness
follows steam.
I'm sure as sweat
that follows heat.
The bead
of sweat that
follows steam.
I'm sure as heat,
as surety.
The bleed
and heave of surety.

——

I'm in the midst
of sureness,
sure as bricks.
I'm sure as cold
that follows
wetness follows
mist. The blood
and heft of sureness,
sure as mud.
I'm sure as blood
that follows
wetness follows

sweat. As sure
as heat that follows
wetness follows wet.

————

I'm in the mist
of sureness,
sure as steam.
The hiss and scream
of sureness,
sure as mist.
I'm sure as blood
that follows
meat. I'm sure
as meat.
I'm in the heat
of surety. The bleat
and seethe of surety.
The mist
that follows certainty.

3. LATER FRAGMENTS

[I traveled to expectancy]

I traveled to expectancy
Through expectancy

Feared my way through
Fear my scholarship

Criterion among criterions
I loitered at the wooden

Doors I had a touch
Of something like a flu

A forfeiture of something
In my gut but like a charm

A gendered thing I guess
I wasn't swayed to bring it up

[I remember partially]

I remember partially

My searching
Party going out in search

Of my own
Life my lantern light

Like water sloshing
Down the front

Of me and calling
My own name

Into the forest dusk
A partial sound

A painful braying
Syllable

That grounded
Like a current

In the dirt a yard
In front of me

But I resorted to it
Like a witness does

To memory

And reason followed
Me allowed me

To the depression
In the land

Where I was
Hiding in the wet

My shirt and socks
Soaked through

With mud

And sweat I didn't
Make it easy

On myself I never do

[I tried early moving]

I tried early moving early sleeping early

Before the day could hide away its time

In me could stay my journey stain

My coat but night is so much like day

These days one holed up inside the other

The way desire predators the sloth in me

And the sloth in me predates desire

[I reached an arm]

I reached an arm
Across Louise
And doing so I made

A shape it gave
Me pause a wending
Shape an absent

Mind she said
Goes limb to limb
With the sublime

Our dialogue
Was saucerless
And glassy overgrown

With cultures
Like the sunless pool
Of water ponding

Underneath
Our garden chairs
A multiplying

Trawl of stillnesses
Wisdom-less
And gold with fish

She said and this
Is where I stayed
My listening

To scratch an itch
Of shame
A goldfish pond

Is mostly water
Little gold in it at all
Despite its name

[Why the dead]

Why the dead
This woman Jean

Come after me
Distended

In their crowns
I don't know why

The dead come
After me in

Crowds of Jeans
Proclaiming

That the god
Of death before

The door to life
Was shut

Slipped out
Into the slapping

Rain today is Easter
Sunday

And I'm reading
Jean again

[I had a little]

I had a little
Intuition left in me

Endured on
Broth I boiled
Off the bones
Of intuition

\

It's a dirty
Game to go on
Intuition only

To follow
Intuition like a dog
Across the sluices
And sands

To leave
My slurried
Footprints
In the sulfur

\

A juried thing
A ceremony
Bound to do
Its civil duty

To lay the bread
Of intuition
At the feet
Of beauty

Tell you what
This intuition
Assuaged every
One but me

[Am I indulgent]

Am I indulgent
Yes
As snow

Indulges
In capacity

Endeavors
To be sexless

Fails
And sticks
To everything

/

If I am
Indulgent tell
Me how

To put this
Causal
Impulse down

Back in its
Spring-
Loaded box

Like snow
Surveils
The hemisphere

Sees us naked
Pauses in
Embarrassment

/

I am indulgent
Yet

Recompense
Of mind
Or so they say

Like snow
Is not a choice

[Without work]

Without work
I'm still
Sure work will come

It always does
Like flu

Expects to find
A lung
Or drought

The desultory
Ember

In the stove-
Lengths

And the leaves
I hope
For accident

To be bowled
Down pat
Dry sent home

Where work
Will wait

For me
Expectantly

Behind
The eaves
And wave its

Broken plank
At me

4. ON INVENTION

On Invention

1.

In *De Inventione*, Cicero suggests "that which is concerned in
the discussion and explanation of things has three parts: fable,
history, and argument." Fables, he says, are statements that are
"neither true nor probable." His example: "Huge winged snakes,
join'd by one common yoke." "History," rather, is "an account
of exploits which have been performed, removed from the
recollection of our own age: [. . .] 'Appius declared war against
the Carthaginians.'" "Argument," he says, "is an imaginary case,
which still might have happened."

2.

In the fable of my life, my brother was born an addict, crested into this world with blue lips, sucking the fentanyl lollipop. When he came forth, the world was already full of me. In my early memories, I argue with myself not to stab my own eye with a kitchen knife; I pick at the fragile, taut skin over my larynx until it bleeds and scabs — rituals to stave off this other girl, whose dark ideas often seem sane and rational: the imaginary case. Our history is that my brother started using young. I became the child sister of the child addict. The children of the parents of an addict. The argument: teenagers, aging backwards. Huge winged snakes joined by a common yoke.

3.

I found the full text to Cicero's *De Inventione*, which he wrote
between 91 and 88 BC, online while searching for the transcript
of a story I heard on NPR about the future of food processing.
"The rift between the reinvention camp and the deinvention
camp has existed for decades," explained journalist Amanda
Little. "One side covets the past, the other side covets the
future." The word "deinvention" caught my ear, so I Googled
it. Cicero's text was the first viable result, under a music video
and "Try this search again with *reinvention*?" Deinvention. An
invented word, signifying the opposite. *De Inventione*. When
a word emerges from the ether like a tender cotyledon, I snip
it up.

4.

I tried to use it in a poem. "Deinvention," I thought, was an apt and complicated metaphor for a tubal ligation procedure I am considering: the "deinvention" of an ideal of womanhood tied to mothering, of personhood tied to parenting. The poem was not viable, but I have collected it here in a pail:

> Call it deinvention
> Little big procedure
> Of the mind —
>
>> As if a fable came
>> Unstitched within
>> Me by a hand
>> Beneath the table

5.

My mother was also the child sister of a child addict. Before me, three generations have parented addict sons — Mildred, Ann, and Lynn each spending their lives with their horns locked to their sons' horns, in love and in agony. My decision to abstain from parenthood (a privilege I do not take for granted) is locked, in part, to this argument. But this history, unlike Cicero's definition, is undetached. Abject. Attached to my recollection. Early memories shadowed by later ones. In the fable of my family, addiction is passed from hand to hand like a hot coal. My brother holds it, palm open.

6.

When I tried an IUD, I bled down my legs as I was led to the ultrasound room. They pressed the device against me and told me it was normal. When I still had pain a month later, they told me it was normal to have pain for a month. To have pain for three months. To have pain for up to a year. Their argument: to "give it time" — the imaginary case. When I had it removed, I wept. It landed on a silver tray with a wet resonance. Deinvention. I got on the pill, which made my periods worse. That's abnormal, the nurses told me. As if a fable came unstitched within me by a hand beneath the table.

7.

I invent a future version of myself who changes her mind about
parenting. Knife gestating knife. But she's unviable. I deinvent
her, close the leather book. I unhook her from her wooden yoke.
From her brother, from her uncles. From her mothers. *You don't
want a child like your brother,* a therapist asks without asking.
But what about if you have a child like you? A girl, tethered to her
silence. Spelling, by accident, "ligation" as "litigation" on my
consultation request form — a little on the nose. In the fable of
my life, I was born childless. History congeals into fable, and
fable, argument. One side covets the past, the other the future.

5. HAIBUN

On moving

Like butter, gone. I'm moving on, because it would be ludicrous
to stay. It feels like a return (to sanity), although I've never been.
(I've never lived a mile west of Illinois.) "I come home from the
soaring," Rilke writes, which I take as imperative (omit the "I"):
to ground, return to Earth, to grind the fable of my life down
like orpiment into a yellow ash and tie my body to the floor.
Rilke writes of God ("still roaring in my ears") but God, for me
(today) is fear. Goodbye to my deteriorating house. Delirium. I'm
out the door. Stasis is a sieve through which I drag myself.

Literature feels / far away. Black bulls grazing / beyond a pale hill.

On poetry

I know a little poetry. It frightens me. The way it breaks, the way experience breaks in. Or it breaks out: like mold on plums, a ring of rash around the mouth, or wilderness — bluestem blanketing the earth, then breaking down to dirt. I know a little poetry. I've broken down. I've wept into the zenith of a rose. "Each tear [. . .] A globe." The way John Donne rhymes "wind" and "find" in the final stanza of OF WEEPING. I've come that close.

Ars poetica: / Yelling "representative" / into a dead line.

On breath

I am under-interpreting my symptoms, the doctor says. My
interpretation can no longer be trusted. I'm seated in a glass
spirometry machine. On one monitor, green lines tick against a
dark backdrop. On another, a cursor draws roulettes. It will feel
like you're breathing with your mouth against a brick wall, the
doctor says. Air buckles behind my lips. So in love with interpre-
tation, I'm blue in the face from kissing it.

I've grown accustomed / to, even fond of, these brief / condi-
tions, reliefs.

On theatre

I wrote a play, out cold in urgent care. Heated blankets toweling my sweated hair. When staged, the actress playing Mother held a wicker broom for acts two and three, with which she beat and beat the rug — a heavy tapestry rolled across the deck. It jumped with fleas — a cast of tiny specks that leapt with urgent hunger as she swept. Lucidly, I slept. I always do, when in duress (no escape from the world of the page). So I wondered how I would create the effect on stage — what props and practical effects — and who would clean up the mess?

I quit theatre / because it spoiled other / darknesses for me.

On dreaming

I walk across the wide array of teeming arrow barns. A hundred
teeming prefab barns with silver hoop-house roofs. Inside, a
hundred-thousand horses, decommissioned for the evening of
their gleaming, crib their crooked teeth against their stalls. And
then, a docent wind, and I'm standing in the centriole. Error
garden. Its treasure guarded by a foal.

I sleep like sleep is / water. Sleeping lugged around / in steel
canteens.

On knowing

What I didn't know grew over what I knew. Like sober news
from home, it sobered me. It touched down like a flea of doubt
touched down on me. And bit. So suddenly, like tardy students
at the door, a little sadness on their faces as they make their plea.
My grace, a sham, a fraying pillowcase.

Helicopter seeds. / Annunciation amid / Iowa weather.

On beauty

"At least two poets," hordes of them, Brand writes in WINTER
EPIGRAMS, "one hundred other women that I know," (a pause)
"and I," (the poem breaks: and I) "can't wait to become old and
haggard." "Can't wait," she writes, an absolute. Ribbon turning
back to string. "Then we don't have to [. . .] sidle up to any-
thing." "Don't" she writes, instead of "won't" — and shows her
hand — the future tense unravels, comes unmanned. "Don't,"
imperative, a beautiful demand. Her "we," like poetry. We come
uncouth. Truth is beauty; beauty isn't truth.

Haggard already, / I slip my bridle. Sidle / up and out of youth.

On growth

I have a worm beneath my hair — a future worm, a nerve from
the eternal present. Crawled out of a wedding urn. My worm has
no utility — a boiled-looking, ruddy thing — he made a home of
incongruency. Emily — "He fathomed me —" Not self, or buzzéd
self. Not self strung out on beauty. But my worm, afraid and
unafraid. As lassoed by my string.

I first published this / poem with line breaks. But it / regrew
from cut parts.

On influence

I'm under it. Addicted, too. The family disease. My obsessions
weigh on me. It's loud — the membrane language of the brain
— but plain, like spoken language overheard. Like laudanum and
anchovies to clean the nerve. To ease the rash. To being good.
This paragraph.

If I could think a / single thought that didn't burn / itself to ash,
I / would —

On difficulty

Difficulty is sacred. Even this thought. Like a yawn that fights
its way out from the cochlea. Private as a runny nose. The word
"Say" that begins Kay Ryan's seminal poem: "Say when rain /
cannot make / you more wet." "Say" its own unit of meaning
until "when" arrives, and the unit is transformed. "Say when" is
then tripled by "rain." Tripled by the rain — which rhymes with
the poet's name.

Rhyme is so public. / Weeping openly / in a crowded latitude.

Acknowledgements

Thank you to the hardworking editors, guest editors, judges, and staff at the journals, magazines, anthologies, and other venues where these poems first appeared, sometimes in different versions:

Annulet: A Journal of Poetics: "[I reached an arm];" "[I had a little];" and "[I traveled to expectancy]"

The Adroit Journal: "Ode" (reprinted) and "The Rest" (reprinted)

Best New Poets 2021: 50 Poems from Emerging Writers (Samovar Press/Meridian, 2022): "Six Revisions" (reprinted)

Changes Review: "[Why the dead];" "Public Abstract;" and "[Revision: Sonnet]" (in a different version, titled "[I found a sequence]")

Columbia Journal: "The Mosquito"

Gulf Coast: "On growth" (in a different version, titled "The Worm")

Jewish Currents: "[I tried moving early]"

The Los Angeles Review of Books: "[I had a bout]"

The Massachusetts Review: "[I remember partially];" "[I couldn't drive];" and "[There was a clearance]"

The Nation: "[Am I indulgent]"

The New Yorker: "Ode"

Academy of American Poets Poem-a-Day: "On moving"

Poet Lore: "[I was reticent in childhood]"

The Poetry Society of America: "Three Odes," winner of the 2023 Cecil Hemley Memorial Award

Poetry Magazine: "Six Revisions;" "The Rest;" "Revision;" "Surety;" and "Failed Sestina"

Send Me Press: "On knowing"

Sixth Finch: "[I thought that I could love]"

Typo: "Sestina with Six Titles"

To my teachers at Kalamazoo College, The University of Iowa, and The University of Denver, especially those who took care with my work and helped me build and edit this manuscript. To the scholarship and fellowship programs at these institutions, as well as their donors, funders, and administrators, that made my education possible. To my dearest colleagues and friends at these institutions, who are too numerous to list here but who have helped shape my life and writing. To the proprietors of the Willapa Bay Artist Residence program, where some of these poems were written and edited. To the Poetry Foundation and the stewards, readers, and judges of the Ruth Lilly and Dorothy Sargent Rosenberg Poetry Fellowship, which helped make this book possible. To the editors, guest editors, staff, and judges at the journals, magazines, anthologies, and other venues where these poems first appeared and were reprinted. To my friends in Iowa City, especially those at Prairie Lights and the Magid Center for Undergraduate Writing. To Dana Levin for selecting this book for publication, for her beautiful foreword and blurb, and for her guidance in the editorial process. To the teams at *The American Poetry Review* and Copper Canyon Press for their fastidious work on this book, especially Elizabeth Scanlon and Gopa Campbell.

To Rae Armantrout, for the blurb. To my family and loved ones: Mom, Dad, Grant, Sam, Nina, Jim. To my beloved dogs, past and present. And to Diane Seuss, for the blurb, of course, and for her mentorship. All of my poems are dedicated to you.

Notes:

I owe thanks to all of my conscious and unconscious poetic influences — both in regard to the poetic forms this book employs as well as its content. Notably, the "Haibun" section owes thanks to seventeenth-century Japanese poet Matsuo Bashō, who originated the haibun form. Thank you to poets who have stewarded and practiced this form for generations following Bashō for guiding my study. Thank you also to the inventor of the sestina form — frequently attributed to a troubadour of twelfth-century Provence, Arnaut Daniel — as well as its many practitioners. The sestina was essential to the conception of this book

The book's epigraphs are from Jean Valentine's poem, "Actuarial File," from her book *Door in the Mountain: New and Collected Poems, 1965–2003* (Wesleyan University Press, 2004); and from Louise Bourgeois' installation, "Cell I (1994)," where it appears embroidered in red on a piece of burlap. This quote is credited as originating in Bourgeois' 1991 text, "On Cells," first published as part of a Carnegie International exhibition catalog for the Carnegie Museum. I owe thanks to Ulf Küster's book, *Louise Bourgeois* (Hatje Cantz, 2012), for this helpful context and bibliographical information.

6: "[I was reticent in childhood]" references Louise Bourgeois' 2004 triptych, "The Reticent Child."

16: The second section of "Three Odes" is a modified duplex, a form originated by Jericho Brown.

20: "[My head and its ache]" references Nicolae Tonitza's 1927 painting, "Two Sisters."

28: "Six Revisions" owes credit to and uses lines from *Confessions* by Saint Augustine, translated by Henry Chadwick (Oxford University Press, 1991); a misprint of the Chadwick translation, transcribed on an online resource; and *Augustine of Hippo* by Peter Brown with translations by Michael Walsh (University of California Press, 1967).

36: "Revisions" quotes and makes reference to William Butler Yeats' poem, "A Coat," which I accessed online via the Poetry Foundation.

63: "On Invention" owes credit to "Book I" of Marcus Tullius Cicero's *De Inventione,* translated by C. D. Yonge (1853), which I accessed online via Wikisource; and the NPR story, "Amanda Little: What Is The Future Of Our Food?", a conversation between Amanda Little and Manoush Zomorodi, which aired on the TED Radio Hour on September 3, 2021. Thank you also to my mom and brother for their fact-checking efforts.

73: "On poetry" references and contains lines from John Donne's "A Valediction: of Weeping," which I accessed online via the Poetry Foundation.

74: "On moving" references and contains lines from Rainer Maria Rilke's poem, "Ich komme aus meinen Schwingen heim" ("I come home from the soaring") from *Rilke's Book of Hours: Love Poems to God,* translated by Anita Barrows and Joanna Macy (Riverhead Books, 1996, 83). When this poem was first published, I included an incorrect citation within it, an error which I aim to correct here.

79: "On beauty" references and contains lines from Dionne Brand's poem series, "The Epigrams to Ernesto Cardenal In Defense of Claudia" from *Winter Epigrams and Epigrams to Ernesto Cardenal In Defense of Claudia* (Williams-Wallace International, 1983). I accessed this poem in *Nomenclature: New and Collected Poems* (Duke University Press, 2022, 151), where it is reprinted. This poem also references and uses a line from John Keats' "Ode on a Grecian Urn," which I accessed online via the Poetry Foundation.

80: "On growth" references and uses a quote from Emily Dickinson's poem, "In Winter in my Room," cataloged as J1670 in *The Poems of Emily Dickinson* edited by Thomas H. Johnson (Belknap Press, 1955).

82: "On difficulty" references and uses lines from Kay Ryan's poem, "All Your Horses," first published in *Poetry Magazine* in September 2014 and later in *Erratic Facts* (Grove Press, 2015, 14).

About the Author

JANE HUFFMAN is a doctoral student in poetry at the University of Denver and is a graduate of the Iowa Writers' Workshop. She is editor-in-chief of *Guesthouse*, an online literary journal. Her work has appeared in *The New Yorker, Poetry, The Nation*, and elsewhere. She was a 2019 recipient of the Ruth Lilly and Dorothy Sargent Rosenberg Fellowship from the Poetry Foundation.